Understanding
the Human Body

Understanding the
Brain and the Nervous System

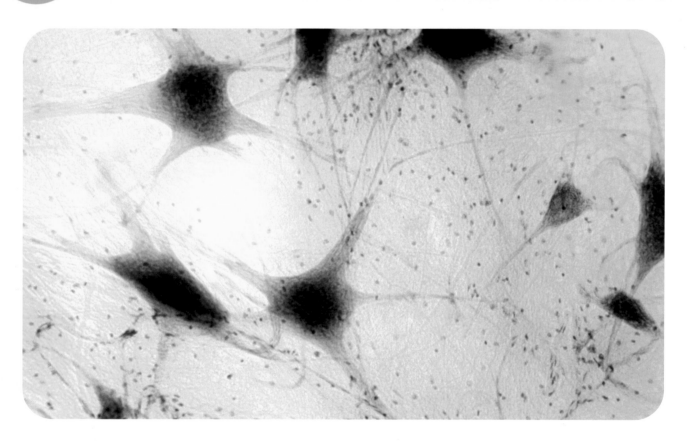

Robert Snedden

New York

Published in 2010 by The Rosen Publishing Group Inc.
29 East 21st Street, New York, NY 10010

First Edition

Library of Congress Cataloging-in-Publication Data

Snedden, Robert.
 Understanding the brain and the nervous system / Robert Snedden. -- 1st ed.
    p. cm. -- (Understanding the human body)
 Includes index.
 ISBN 978-1-4358-9685-7 (library binding)
 ISBN 978-1-4358-9691-8 (paperback)
 ISBN 978-1-4358-9696-3 (6-pack)
 1. Nervous system--Juvenile literature. 2. Brain--Juvenile literature. I. Title.
 QP361.5.S64 2010
 612.8--dc22

                                2009028244

Photo Credits:
Alton Towers: cover and p. 16; Getty Images: title page and p. 8 (Visuals Unlimited), p. 27
(Louie Psihoyos); Istockphoto.com: p. 11 (Mark Evans), p. 26 (Wojciech Krusinski),
p. 29 (Steve Luker), p. 36 (Brad Killer); National Library of Medicine: p. 34; Science
Photo Library: p. 10 (Steve Gschmeissner), p. 12 (Riccards Cassiani-Ingoni),
p. 14 (Steve Gschmeissner), 32 (Innerspace Imaging); Shutterstock: pp. 6
(Olga Bogatyrenko), 18 (L T O'Reilly), p. 20 (Laurence Gough), p. 23
(Stephen Mcsweeny), p. 24 (Daniela Sachsenheimer) p. 28 (Margie
Hurwich), p. 30 (S. Ragets), p. 33 (prism_68), p.35 (Suzanne Tucker),
p.38 (empipe), p.39 (forestpath), p. 40 (Kitch Bain), p. 41 (Four Oaks),
p. 43 (Diego Cervo); University of California, San Diego: p. 37
(Susan F. Tapert Ph.D).

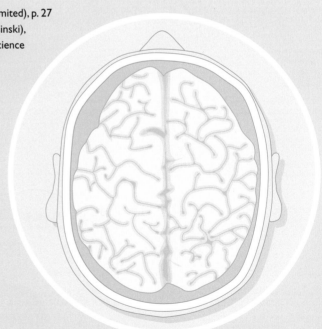

Manufactured in China
CPSIA Compliance Information: Batch #WAW0102YA: For Further Information contact
Rosen Publishing, New York, New York at 1-800-237-9932

Contents

A network of nerves

All through your body there runs an information network of nerves. This nervous system is one of the ways that the body keeps in touch with what is going on in its different parts. It is the means by which you issue instructions to the parts of the body you can control, such as your arms and legs. It also allows other parts of your body, such as your heart, to go on working without you having to think about them.

Neuroanatomy

The study of the nervous system is called neuroanatomy. This looks at the different structures in the nervous system and how they fit together, from the workings of individual nerve cells to the thought centers of the brain. The nervous system has two main divisions. One is called the central nervous system, the other is called the peripheral nervous system.

The central nervous system

Two of the most important parts of the whole nervous system are found in the central nervous system: the brain and the spinal cord. The brain is the body's control center and it is the part that holds your personality.

The spinal cord stretches down your back from your brain, protected by the bones of the spinal column. Nerves extend from the spinal cord, linking up with the peripheral nervous system that runs through the rest of the body. The peripheral nervous system carries information and instructions back and forth from the body's systems to the brain.

The peripheral nervous system

The peripheral nervous system can itself be divided into two parts—the somatic nervous system and the autonomic nervous system.

A tennis player's nervous system has to react quickly to deal with a ball traveling toward him at 87 miles (140 kilometers) per hour.

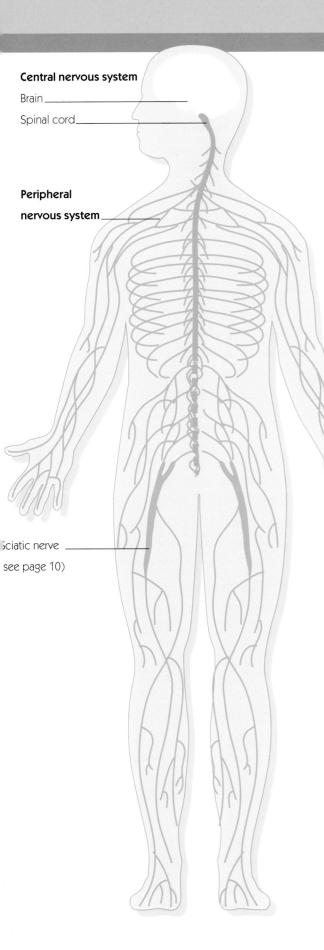

Central nervous system

Brain _____

Spinal cord _____

Peripheral

nervous system _____

Sciatic nerve _____

(see page 10)

◄ *There are two main parts to the human nervous system—the central nervous system and the peripheral nervous system.*

The somatic nervous system carries signals from other parts of the body to the central nervous system. It also carries signals from the central nervous system to trigger muscle movement.

The autonomic nervous system controls movements in parts of the body that are usually not under conscious control. For instance, although you can deliberately hold your breath, the autonomic nervous system keeps you breathing without you being conscious of it the whole time. It also controls the muscles that move food through the digestive system; we do not have to think about moving these muscles at all.

Investigate

Did you know that people once believed that we did our thinking with our hearts? When the Egyptians were making mummies, they carefully kept the person's heart but scooped out the brain and threw it away! However, the Egyptians were also the first people to write about the anatomy of the brain. Find out more about what the Egyptians thought the brain did and how they saw its anatomy.

Nerve cells

Your body is made up of trillions of cells. There are many different types of cell in the human body—each of them specialized to perform a particular function. For example, muscle cells provide the power to move the body, and cells in the digestive system break down and absorb food. The role of the nerve cells is to carry information.

Neurons

Individual nerve cells are called neurons. There are many billions of them in the body, carrying information in pulses of electricity. A neuron can be divided into three main parts: the cell body, dendrites, and axons.

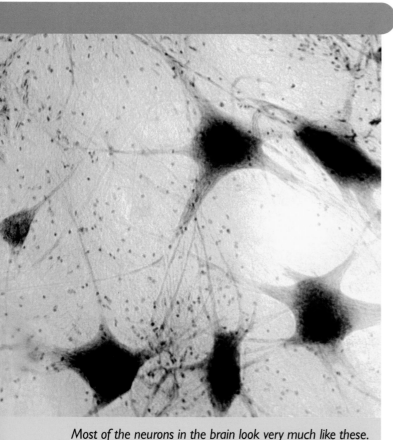

Most of the neurons in the brain look very much like these. Many connections are formed between individual neurons.

The neuron's cell body is similar to that of any other kind of cell. Here we find the nucleus, the cell's control center, which issues chemical instructions to the rest of the cell. The cell body also contains other cell structures that provide the cell with energy and build the proteins it needs.

Dendrites and axons

Stretching out from the neuron are a number of thin extensions. The shortest of these are called dendrites. The name comes from a Greek word meaning "tree," and it describes the branching appearance of the dendrites. Most nerve cells have about six main dendrites. These are the pathways to the cell, bringing in information from other neurons.

The longest of the cell extensions is called the axon, or nerve fiber. This is the pathway leading away from the cell. The axon carries nerve impulses from the cell body, usually to another neuron or to a muscle.

The end of the axon is branched. These branches allow it to pass on nerve impulses to more than one other cell. A single axon can have branches that allow it to make contact with the dendrites or cell bodies of thousands of other cells.

Schwann cells

Longer axons are covered with a fatty sheath, or covering, called myelin. This myelin sheath acts like the insulation around an electrical cable. It helps to ensure that the nerve impulses pass efficiently along the axon. The myelin comes from cells called Schwann cells, which curl themselves around the axon. A number of Schwann cells form a line, like a string of sausages, down the length of the axon.

The synapse

Neurons do not make direct contact with each other. Between the axon of one cell and the dendrite of another, there is a tiny gap called the synapse. At the synapse, the arriving signal causes molecules called neurotransmitters to be released. These neurotransmitters then travel across the gap to the next cell, where they trigger another nerve impulse.

Body facts

A human brain has 100 billion neurons.

A typical neuron has between 1,000 and 10,000 connections to other neurons.

There are probably around 2,000 billion connections in your brain. That is roughly one connection for every second since the dinosaurs became extinct.

▼ Signals are sent from one neuron to another along the axon. Chemicals called neurotransmitters carry the signal across a small gap to the other cell's dendrite or body.

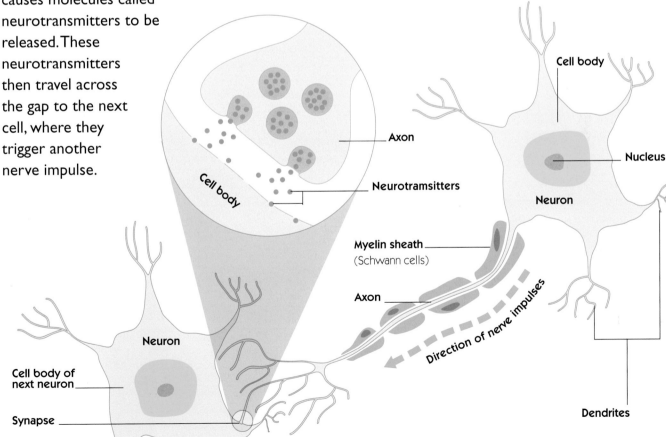

Cell body

Axon

Neurotramsitters

Cell body

Cell body

Nucleus

Neuron

Myelin sheath
(Schwann cells)

Axon

Direction of nerve impulses

Neuron

Cell body of
next neuron

Synapse

Dendrites

Nerve cord networks

Tens of thousands of miles of cordlike nerves pass through every part of your body. They range from the microscopically thin to the 0.5-in. (1-cm) wide sciatic nerves that run from the lower back and down the legs. Together, they provide a network of information that helps keep your body organized and healthy.

Fiber bundles

A nerve is actually made up of a large number of nerve axons, or fibers, each extending from an individual nerve cell body. Each axon is covered by its Schwann cells, which sheath it in myelin. The bundles of nerve fibers are held together inside a tough, protective covering. A large nerve may contain hundreds of thousands of nerve fibers, the thinnest nerves may only have a few.

Two-way traffic

Nerves can be made up of two different types of nerve fiber: sensory nerve fibers and motor nerve fibers. Sensory nerve fibers carry

Body facts

The speed of a nerve impulse varies with the type of signal being sent. The signals for muscle position travel up to 390 feet (119 meters) per second. This way, even with your eyes closed, you know exactly where your hands are all the time. Some pain signals travel slowly, at around 20 inches (0.5 meters) per second. If you stub your toe, you'll feel the impact right away, but you won't feel the pain for another couple of seconds.

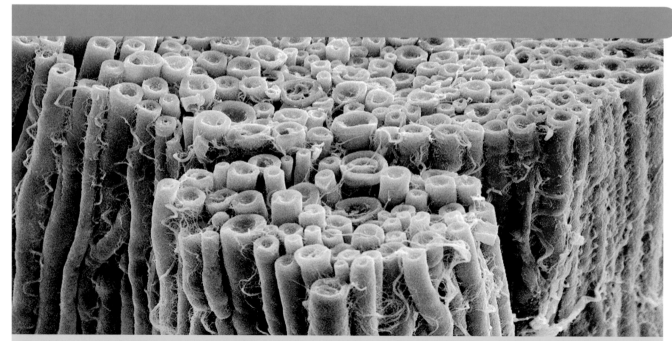

A nerve is made up of a bundle of nerve fibers. Each of the fibers here is an axon from an individual nerve cell.

When driving at high speed, a fast reaction time can make the difference between winning and losing a race.

information from the senses to the central nervous system. Motor nerve fibers carry messages back to the muscles to trigger movement. So if you put your hand on something you don't like the feel of, your brain can instruct your arm muscles to pull your hand away.

The time it takes for information to be sent to the brain via the sensory nerves, for the brain to process this and make a decision, then to send a signal to the muscles to take action, is often referred to as a person's reaction time. Some people, such as fighter pilots, need to have very fast reaction times.

Some nerves carry messages in both directions. In these nerves, the bundles contain sensory fibers and motor fibers. Other nerves only work in one direction. For instance, the nerve that brings information from the nose to the brain about smells has only sensory nerve fibers. There are no motor fibers.

Try this

Test your reaction time by having someone drop a ruler between your outstretched fingers. Then measure how far the ruler fell before you caught it. In this way, you can work out your reaction time. For most people, it is between 0.2 and 0.25 seconds, but we tend to get slower as we get older.

The central nervous system

The central nervous system consists of the brain and spinal cord. It is the body's control center. The spinal cord conducts information from nerves in the rest of the body to the brain, and relays instructions from the brain to the rest of the body. The brain receives input from the spinal cord and other nerve centers that connect to it directly, such as the eyes and nose. It processes this information, then sends out appropriate responses.

Gray matter, white matter

The central nervous system is made up of gray matter and white matter. Gray matter is so-called because it appears grayish in color. It is made up of concentrations of nerve cell bodies clustered close together.

Bundles of axons carrying information between nerve cells make up the white matter. They appear white because this is the color of the myelin that sheathes the axons.

Support cells

The central nervous system is made up of billions of neurons and trillions of glial cells. Glial cells provide support for neurons and repair damage. The brain has between 10 and 50 times as many glial cells as it does neurons. The glial cells provide an essential support network for the neurons, without which they just could not work. The Schwann cells, described earlier on page 9, are a type of glial cell.

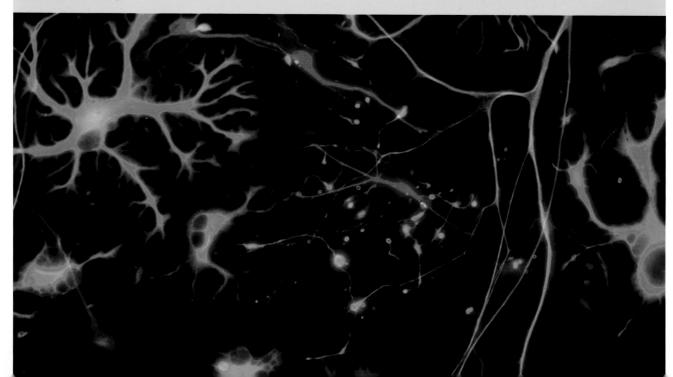

The neurons in the brain rely on a support network of glial cells. In this photograph, glial cells are shown in green and neurons are in red.

These are the different types of glial cell found in the central nervous system and what they do:

• Astroglia transport nutrients to the neurons, remove their waste, and keep them in place

• Oligodendroglia provide the myelin insulation for cells in the central nervous system—the same job that the Schwann cells do elsewhere

• Microglia digest parts of worn-out neurons.

The meninges

The brain and spinal cord are protected by three layers of connective tissues. These layers are together known as the meninges. The two inner layers are filled by a clear and colorless liquid called cerebrospinal fluid. This helps to cushion the brain and spinal cord. It also carries waste products into the bloodstream for removal.

Investigate

Infections of the meninges lead to the serious illness called meningitis. This is a life-threatening condition that isn't always easy to detect right away. It can be caused by infections of bacteria, viruses, and fungi. Symptoms can include headaches and fevers, vomiting and muscle pains. See what you can find out about what is being done to treat and prevent this serious condition.
A good way to start would be to look at websites of some meningitis organizations.

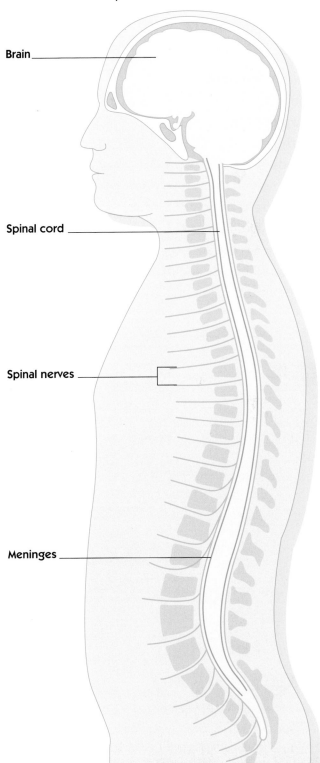

▼ The brain and spinal cord together make up the central nervous system.

Brain

Spinal cord

Spinal nerves

Meninges

The spinal cord

The spinal cord is a thick bundle of nerves that forms the main information pathway between the brain and the peripheral nervous system. It is protected by the spinal column, or backbone. The spinal cord passes through the spinal canal, a tunnellike space at the center of the backbone.

Spinal segments

The spinal cord is divided into 31 segments. Starting from the neck, there are 8 cervical, 12 thoracic, 5 lumbar, and 5 sacral segments. It ends in a single coccygeal segment.

The pattern of gray and white matter changes in different segments of the spinal cord. This is because the concentration of nerve cell bodies and axon bundles varies between the segments.

In the cervical segments, there is quite a lot of white matter. This is because there are many axons here, traveling up to the brain from all the way down the spinal cord. Lower down in the sacral segments, there is not so much white matter. This is because there are fewer axons passing through these segments.

Differences can also be seen in the amount of gray matter in the spinal segments. For example, there is a lot of gray matter in the cervical segments. This is because they are packed with motor neurons that control the arms and legs.

Spinal nerves

A pair of spinal nerves emerge from each spinal cord segment. These carry information to the rest of the body from the spinal cord and back from the body up to the brain. The spinal nerves are grouped according to the spinal cord segments they emerge from. The cervical nerves deal with movement and feeling in the neck, arms, and upper body. Thoracic nerves deal

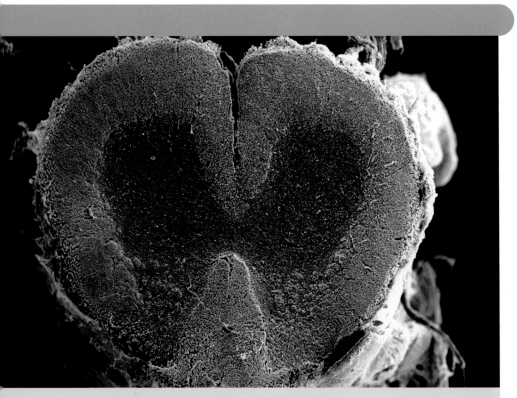

This photograph shows a cross section through the spinal cord. The gray matter is shown in red and the white matter in yellow. The thin layer on the outside is the meninges.

with the lower body and abdomen, and lumbar and sacral nerves deal with the legs, bladder, bowels, and sexual organs. The coccygeal nerves are small nerves that carry sensory messages from the skin around the coccyx (tailbone).

Horse's tail

The spinal column is actually quite a bit longer than the spinal cord. In men, the spinal cord is about 17.7 in. (45 cm) in length. In women, it is about 16.9 in. (43 cm). This means that the nerves branching out from the lower parts of the spinal cord—the lower lumbar, sacral, and coccygeal nerves—run through the spinal column before they leave it. Because of their appearance, this collection of nerves running through the spinal canal are called the cauda equina, a name that means "horsetail."

Body facts

Both humans and giraffes have the same number of cervical vertebrae (neck bones) in their necks—a giraffe's are just much bigger than yours. Although there are a few exceptions to this rule, most mammals have seven neck bones. Two of the exceptions are the slow-moving sloths of the South American rainforest. Two-toed sloths have six cervical vertebrae, and three-toed sloths have nine.

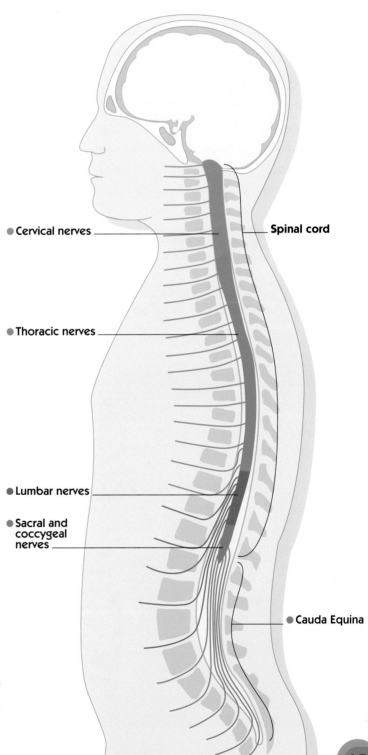

▼ *Different parts of the spinal cord are shown here in different colors. Thirty-one pairs of nerves spread out from the spinal cord.*

● Cervical nerves ———————————— **Spinal cord**

● Thoracic nerves

● Lumbar nerves

● Sacral and coccygeal nerves

● Cauda Equina

The peripheral nervous system

The peripheral nervous system carries information to the central nervous system from the rest of the body. It carries signals from the central nervous system to the muscles and also controls those muscles that aren't under conscious control. The peripheral nervous system is made up of the somatic and autonomic nervous systems.

The somatic nervous system

Somatic means "of the body." The somatic nervous system relays information and instructions back and forth between the central nervous system and the muscles we control by thinking about it. For example, if you want to move your arm, you do it by sending signals along the pathways of the somatic nervous system. A cell body located either in the brain or in the spinal cord has an axon that extends directly to the muscle that it controls.

The autonomic nervous system

Autonomic means "self controlling." The autonomic nervous system regulates activities in the body without us having to think about them. It is made up of a network of control centers and signals.

Information goes through the autonomic nervous system in a two-step process. Instead of a single nerve fiber going directly from the central nervous system to a target muscle, the autonomic system uses two neurons. The first neuron extends from the central nervous system to a nerve cell body in an autonomic ganglion. The ganglion is a collection of neuron cell bodies that acts as a nerve junction point. A second axon extends out from the nerve cell in the ganglion to connect with the target muscle.

Fight or flight

One part of the autonomic nervous system is the sympathetic nervous system. It plays an important role when we are in stressful situations. These are sometimes called "fight

When we feel excitement or fear, the sympathetic nervous system is preparing the body for action.

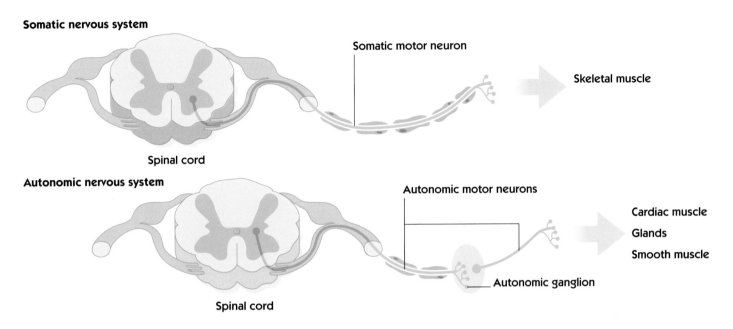

Somatic nervous system

Somatic motor neuron

Skeletal muscle

Spinal cord

Autonomic nervous system

Autonomic motor neurons

Cardiac muscle

Glands

Smooth muscle

Autonomic ganglion

Spinal cord

▲ *The somatic system uses only one neuron to send an instruction to a target muscle, but the autonomic system uses two.*

or flight" situations, because the body has to make itself ready either to fight the danger or to run away from it. When there is danger, the sympathetic nervous system prepares the body for it in the following ways:

• It widens the airways in the lungs so more oxygen is taken in

• It slows down the passage of food through the digestive system

• It directs more blood to the brain

• It reduces blood flow to the skin and internal organs

• It increases muscle tension

• It speeds up the heartbeat.

You will have felt these effects if, for instance, a large dog barks at you unexpectedly. When the danger is over, the parasympathetic nervous system takes over. This slows down the heart rate and returns things to normal.

Investigate

A neurological disorder is a disease or injury to the nervous system that prevents it from working properly. Common neurological disorders include spinal injuries resulting from accidents, multiple sclerosis, strokes, and Parkinson's disease. Do you know of anyone who has one of these conditions and how their lives have been affected? What can be done to help them? See what you can find out.

Making a move

The body is never idle—even when you are asleep it has things to do. The body performs two main types of action: voluntary actions and involuntary actions. Voluntary actions are those that we know about and consciously control, such as throwing a ball. Involuntary actions are those that go on all the time without us thinking about them, such as breathing and digestion. Both types of action are controlled by the nervous system.

The motor cortex

If you decide to get something done, then it starts off as a burst of activity in the cells of the brain. The part of the brain that is important in this is called the motor cortex.

Different zones of the motor cortex are responsible for sending signals to different parts of the body. There are areas that control the lips and tongue, the hands and fingers, the legs and arms, and so on. Some of these areas are bigger than others. For example, the area controlling the fingers is much bigger than the area controlling the legs. This is because the fingers require much more delicate control.

Signals travel from the motor cortex down through the spinal cord. They then travel out into the peripheral nervous system to reach their target muscles.

When the starter gun goes off, this athlete will start running and his nervous system will ensure that his muscles work in a coordinated way.

Monitoring movement

It is important to know that the actions you wanted to take actually happened. Information about the movements of the body is sent back to sites in the brain so that any adjustments can be made. Even when you're sitting absolutely still, little correcting muscle movements have to be made to hold you in position.

Reflex actions

Reflex actions are a type of action that is carried out without thinking. They usually involve a sudden movement, such as snatching your hand away from a hot surface. Reflex actions are quick because they need no conscious instruction from the brain to be carried out. They are literally done without thinking. Only a few nerves are involved—sometimes only three—which also speeds up the response time.

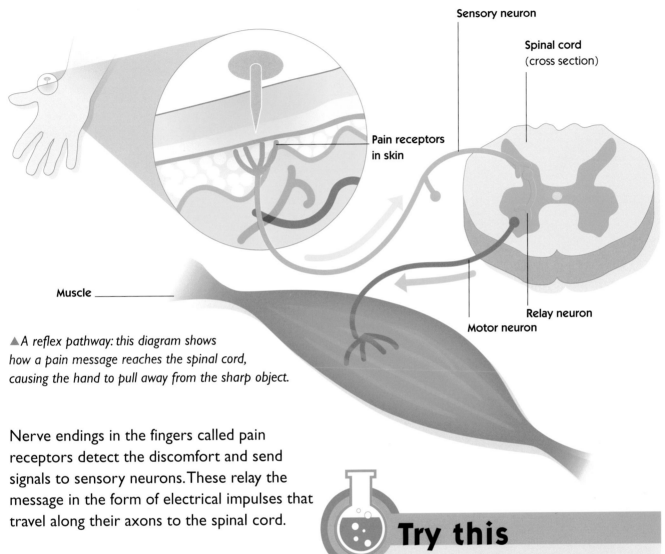

Sensory neuron

Spinal cord
(cross section)

Pain receptors
in skin

Relay neuron

Motor neuron

Muscle

▲ *A reflex pathway: this diagram shows how a pain message reaches the spinal cord, causing the hand to pull away from the sharp object.*

Nerve endings in the fingers called pain receptors detect the discomfort and send signals to sensory neurons. These relay the message in the form of electrical impulses that travel along their axons to the spinal cord.

In the spinal cord, the sensory neurons are linked to relay neurons. If there is a strong enough signal from the sensory neurons, the relay neurons are triggered and they then send the signal on to motor neurons. The motor neurons are responsible for triggering contractions (shortening or tensing) of the muscles that move the arm. This results in the arm jerking away from the danger. The relay neurons also send signals to the brain so you know what just happened. This also helps you to learn not to put your hand on any more hot surfaces!

Try this

Have a friend stand on one side of a window while you go to the other side. Now throw a scrunched up ball of paper, or something else that won't do any damage, at your friend's face. It is almost certain that your friend will blink. People in this situation will blink even though they know that the paper ball cannot hurt them. This is called the blink reflex and it is an important protector of our eyes.

The brain

The average human brain weighs about 3 pounds (1.4 kilograms). It is pinkish-gray in color, and looks a little like a big, wrinkly walnut. If you could flatten out the folds of the brain, its surface would cover an area of 21.5 square feet (2 sq. m). It is made up of billions of neurons that are joined together by trillions of connections.

The forebrain

The largest and most complex part of the brain is called the forebrain. The outer wrinkled part of the forebrain is called the cerebral cortex. It varies in thickness from 0.07–0.2 in. (2–6 mm) and is made up of gray matter. The cortex is where our intelligence, memory, feelings, speech centers, and personality are found—as well as the centers that control movement.

Our knowledge, intelligence, emotions, and decision-making abilities are all stored in our brains.

The cerebrum

One of the main structures of the forebrain is the cerebrum. The cerebrum is divided into right and left hemispheres. Each hemisphere is divided into four parts, known as the frontal, parietal, temporal, and occipital lobes.

Each lobe is responsible for processing different types of information:

• The frontal lobe deals with movement, planning and problem solving, reasoning, emotion, and speech

• The parietal lobe deals with sensory information to do with pain, temperature, touch, and pressure

• The temporal lobe deals with hearing, memory, and perception

• The occipital lobe deals with vision.

Other forebrain structures

Other important parts of the forebrain include the hypothalamus, the thalamus, and the limbic system.

• The hypothalamus takes care of functions we don't think about, such as the body's water balance. Signals from the hypothalamus trigger feelings of thirst. It also regulates when we eat and sleep, and plays a part in displaying emotion.

- The thalamus is a relay center. It routes information from the senses to the cerebral cortex.

- The limbic system is sometimes called "the emotional brain." It is involved in emotion, memory, decision-making, and learning.

From right to left

Each brain hemisphere controls the opposite side of the body, so the right side of the brain controls the muscles on the left side of the body. Sensory information also crosses over to the opposite half of the brain. This means that

Body facts

The human brain accounts for about 2 percent of the weight of the body, but it gets 20 percent of the blood supply from the heart. It also takes up 20 percent of the oxygen we breath in. However, it is not true that you lose heat faster from your head than any other part of your body. That is just a myth.

if one half of the brain is damaged, the effects will be seen on the opposite side of the body. The left and right hemispheres of the brain are linked together by a bridge of 100 million nerve fibers called the corpus callosum.

Cerebrum

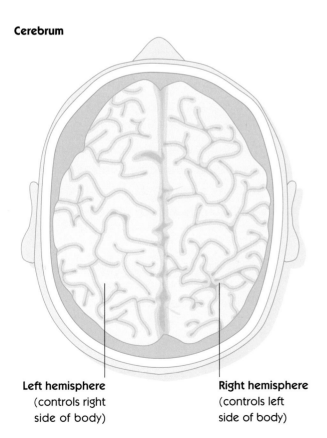

Left hemisphere (controls right side of body)

Right hemisphere (controls left side of body)

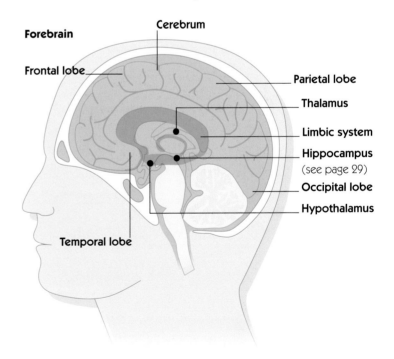

Forebrain

Cerebrum

Frontal lobe

Parietal lobe

Thalamus

Limbic system

Hippocampus (see page 29)

Occipital lobe

Hypothalamus

Temporal lobe

◄▲ *On the left is a view of the cerebrum, as seen from above. It is one of the structures that makes up the forebrain, the part of the brain shown above in green.*

The midbrain and hindbrain

Although the cerebral cortex is where all your thinking goes on, the brain has a number of other very important structures. In the midbrain and the hindbrain are control centers for activities such as breathing and digestion, and for skills we perform without thinking once we've learned them, such as hitting a tennis ball or riding a bike.

The midbrain

The midbrain is a fairly small region of the brain that is about 0.75 inches (2 cm) long. It is found underneath the middle of the forebrain. Two large bundles of nerve fibers travel through the midbrain carrying signals between the cerebral cortex, the brainstem, and the spinal cord. The midbrain also deals with the signals that come from the eyes and ears. It is responsible for controlling eye movement and the automatic opening and closing of the pupils.

The hindbrain

The hindbrain is located beneath and to the rear of the cerebrum. It is divided into three parts:

• The cerebellum

• The pons

• The medulla.

The word *cerebellum* means "little brain." Like the cerebrum, it is divided into hemispheres that are surrounded by a cortex. The cerebellum is responsible for balance, movement, and coordination. It is especially involved in performing skilled actions, such as those needed for playing sports. For example, it is involved in making the split-second adjustments to muscle contractions that allow a tennis player to strike the ball quickly and accurately.

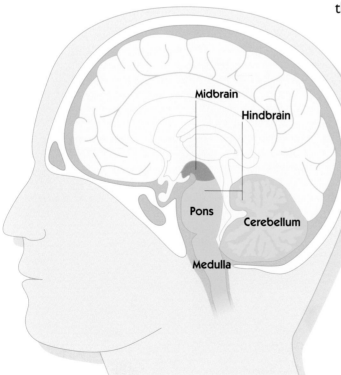

◄ *The midbrain and the main structures of the hindbrain. The midbrain is the green area and the hindbrain is the orange area.*

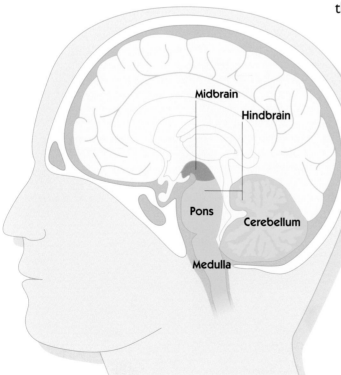

Midbrain
Hindbrain
Pons
Cerebellum
Medulla

The brainstem

The pons and medulla, together with the midbrain, form the brainstem. This is a sticklike structure that emerges from the bottom of the brain and connects it to the spinal cord. The brainstem coordinates all of the brain's messages to other parts of the body. It also controls body functions we are not consciously aware of, such as breathing and digestion.

A part of the brainstem called the pyramids controls skilled movements. In front of this is the pons, which links the cerebellum to the cerebrum. The pons controls sleep and dreams. The medulla forms the lower part of the brainstem. Its job is to control important unconscious functions— e.g., heartbeat, breathing, and blood pressure.

Body facts

When someone falls in love, the brain produces a chemical called phenylethylamine. This gives a feeling of well-being and contentment. It also increases alertness.

The chemical phenylethylamine is also found in chocolate. In addition, chocolate contains a chemical called tryptophan. Tryptophan can lift a person's mood and can produce feelings of happiness. So when you hear someone say that they love chocolate, they probably do!

Part of the hindbrain called the pyramids sends signals from the brain to the muscles that are involved in skilled movements.

Brainwaves

Electrical impulses constantly pass between the cells of the brain as they communicate with each other. The voltages involved are small, no more than a few millions of a volt, but this activity can be detected using sensitive detectors placed on the scalp. The variations in the brain's electrical activity are recorded on a chart called an electroencephalogram (EEG), which shows the changing activity as a series of waves. The height of the wave indicates the strength of the impulse.

Understanding the waves

Doctors can use the information from EEGs to help them find out if the brain is functioning normally. There are four different types of wave, known as alpha, beta, theta, and delta waves. The type of wave produced depends on the activity of the brain at the time. These waves vary in amplitude (height) and frequency. Brainwave frequency is usually measured in hertz—the number of waves per second.

High-frequency, low-amplitude brainwaves are seen when a person is awake and alert. If the person is not concentrating on anything, the brainwave frequency becomes lower. Generally, the more relaxed a person is, the greater the amplitude and the lower the frequency of the brainwaves they produce.

Wave types

Here are different types of brainwaves and the activities that produce them.

Beta waves frequencies ranging from 13 to 60 hertz. These are produced when we are alert and are the waves produced in the normal waking state. The higher frequencies are produced when we are tense, agitated, or afraid.

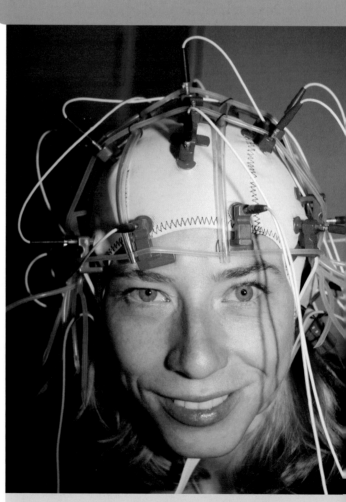

Sensor pads can be placed on the scalp to detect brainwaves. These brainwaves can then be recorded as an electroencephalogram.

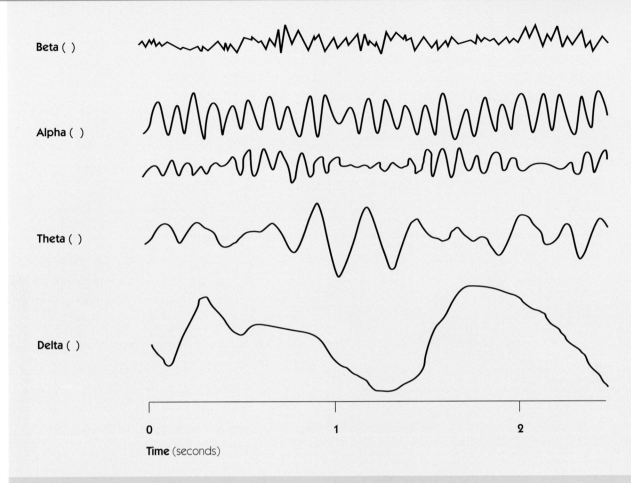

Beta ( )

Alpha ( )

Theta ( )

Delta ( )

Time (seconds)

0   1   2

These are patterns of the four main types of brainwave—beta, alpha, theta, and delta.

Alpha waves frequencies ranging from 7 to 13 hertz. These are produced when we are aware of what is going on but are physically and mentally relaxed.

Theta waves frequencies ranging from 4 to 7 hertz. These are produced when we are feeling drowsy and daydreaming. They may also be associated with creativity.

Delta waves frequencies ranging from 0–1 to 4 hertz. These brainwaves are the slowest in frequency and the highest in amplitude. We produce delta waves when we are in a state of deep sleep or unconsciousness.

Biofeedback

Biofeedback is a procedure by which a person can learn to control activities in the body that are not normally under conscious control. For instance, while an EEG is being made of a person's brainwave patterns, the machine can be made to flash or beep when certain waves are made. These beeps are the feedback.

After a time, the person receiving the feedback can learn to make the machine beep continuously by producing the right kind of brainwaves. These techniques are used to help people deal with stress. They may also be used to help people with epilepsy control their seizures.

Sleeping and dreaming

When we go to sleep, conscious thought appears to cease for a while. We become unaware of what is happening in the world around us, unless there is a stimulus that is strong enough to wake us up, such as a loud noise. While we are asleep, we are obviously vulnerable, or defenseless. But we continue to put ourselves at risk in this way because we can't do without sleep.

We spend around one-third of our lives sleeping. To stay healthy, it is essential that we get enough sleep.

Why do we sleep?

There is no doubt that we need to sleep. Depriving people of sleep is a form of torture that leaves them confused and exhausted. Sleep may be the time when the brain does its "housework," shutting down neurons while repairs are carried out. Sleep is also a way of conserving energy in the body.

In children, growth hormones are released during deep sleep. These are chemicals that control growth of the body. In this way, the body has a chance to build new cells while activity is reduced elsewhere.

Sleep stages

Sleep can be broken down into four main stages. These stages can be shown by activity in the brain recorded on an EEG.

Stage 1 A light sleep, where you are "nodding off"—drifting in and out of sleep and drowsy wakefulness. Muscle activity slows down. Many people experience sudden muscle contractions and a sensation of falling in this stage.

Stage 2 Eye movements stop and brainwave frequency slows, although there may be occasional bursts of rapid wave activity. The body temperature drops.

Investigate

Here are some of the most common things that people say they dream about:

1. Falling

2. Being pursued or attacked

3. Trying to perform a task but repeatedly failing

4. Work and school activities.

Does any of it mean anything? Perhaps—perhaps not! People have always been fascinated by dreams and there have been some weird and wonderful ideas about them. See what you can figure out about your own dreams. Keep a dream diary by your bed and write down any dreams you remember when you wake up.

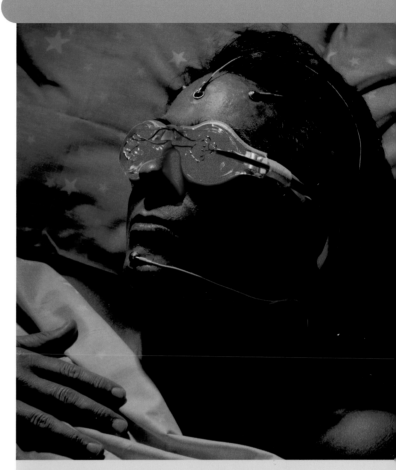

This researcher is studying dreams. The goggles he is wearing detect the beginning of REM sleep, the stage associated with dreaming.

Stage 3 Extremely slow delta waves (low-frequency waves) are produced, interrupted by bursts of faster waves.

Stage 4 The deepest level of sleep, when the brain and the body's main muscles are at their most inactive. It is very difficult to wake a person from sleep stages 3 and 4.

REM

After about 90 minutes of deep sleep, we enter a lighter state of sleep. This state is known as REM or rapid eye movement sleep. It is the time when dreams take place. Our eyes, hands, and feet may become active when we dream. Also, our breathing and heart rate may speed up. Brainwaves during dreaming sleep look like those seen in a person who is awake.

Infants spend almost half of their time asleep in REM sleep. Adults spend only about 20 percent of their sleeping time in REM. This suggests that the dreaming process plays a vital part in learning and forming new connections in the brain.

Memory

As well as controlling activities in the body, the brain is also the place where our memories are stored. Without the brain's huge capacity for storing information as well as processing it, we would never be able to learn anything.

Memory connections

Memories appear to be stored in connections between neurons in the brain. Some memories last longer than others. How long they may last depends on how permanent the connections between the neurons are.

Short-term memory is for things we only need to remember for a short time, such as a phone number we only use once. Things that we need to remember again and again, such as our own phone number, are stored in long-term memory.

For a long-term memory, the neuron connections that are formed are set aside. Remembering "refreshes" the memory. Perhaps it does this by triggering the neuron connections and reminding the brain not to reuse them for something else.

Types of memory

There are different types of memories. There are memories that are conscious, such as remembering what happened at your last birthday party. Other memories are unconscious. Remembering how to ride a bike is an unconscious memory.

Semantic memory is a special type of memory that involves recollecting words and language. Episodic memory concerns events that took place at a certain time, such as a party.

This musician's brain stores the memory of where to place her fingers to make the sounds she wants.

28

Working memory is what the brain uses to keep track of events that are happening now. It allows you to recall where you are moment by moment. You also use working memory to monitor the changing information that is coming to you from your senses. It is this type of memory that tells you when something has changed in your surroundings.

As we get older, we may become more forgetful and find it harder to remember things.

The hippocampus

The brain processes memory in a structure called the hippocampus (see illustration on page 21). If a person's hippocampus is damaged in an accident, they become unable to form new memories, although their memories of past events remain unaffected. They can, however, learn new skills.

The hippocampus appears to take memories, and make connections between them and different memories. For instance, the memory of the warmth of a summer's day may be linked with the memory of a cool ice cream you enjoyed that same day.

These linked memories may then be moved from the hippocampus into the cortex, where they are placed in long-term storage. Links between memories mean that when one is triggered, so are the others. When you taste the ice cream, you remember the summer's day.

Body facts

Briton Daniel Tammet has a truly astonishing memory. He knows 7 languages, one of which (Icelandic) he learned in a week. He can recite numbers of over 20,000 digits with ease and says that he recalls numbers by the pictures they make in his mind. For instance, 37 is porridgy and 89 is like falling snow!

Senses and the brain

Our major sense organs of sight, hearing, taste, and smell are all located in our heads, near the brain. Dedicated areas of the brain are responsible for interpreting and acting upon the flood of information that comes from the eyes, ears, and other sense organs.

Eyes on the world

Every time you look around you, your eyes send a barrage of nerve signals to the brain. These signals travel along the optic nerve, passing through the optic chiasma. This is where the optic nerves split in two and cross over each other. It ensures that signals from both eyes reach both of the brain's visual centers. These centers are known as the primary and secondary visual cortices.

Some of the optic nerves reach the lateral geniculate bodies, midway through the brain. The nerve cells there respond to color and motion. They begin the process of analyzing what we see. Then they route the information to the primary and secondary visual cortices, located toward the back of the brain. The visual cortices analyze the information they have received and make sense of it, giving us a picture of the world we see.

Searching for the sound

Sound waves are made up of a series of vibrations. These vibrations are converted by the ears into electrical impulses. Then the impulses are sent to the brain's auditory cortices, areas located on the sides of the cerebral cortex. This is where the patterns of nerve signals are decoded and compared with sounds previously heard.

Signals from high-pitched sounds generally go to the rear of the auditory cortex. Low-pitched sounds go to the front. An area around the auditory cortex, called the association area, links sounds to other memories, such as the face of the person speaking.

Smells

Odor molecules entering the nose stimulate special sensory cells in the roof of the nasal

Optical illusions trick the brain into "seeing" something that isn't actually there or make things that are static appear to be moving, such as this spiral.

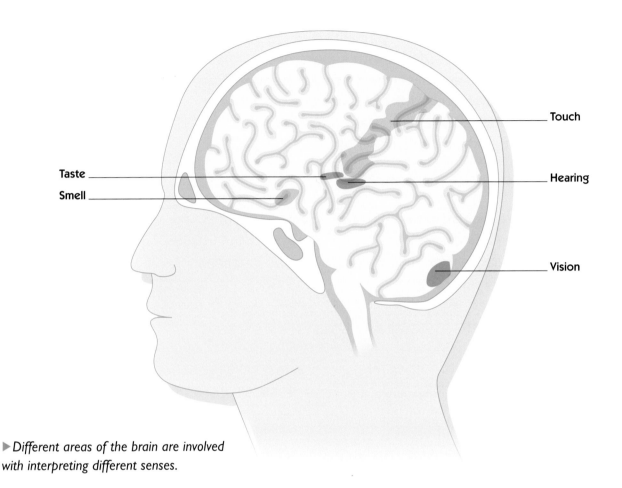

▶ *Different areas of the brain are involved with interpreting different senses.*

Touch

Taste
Smell

Hearing

Vision

cavity. The signals they generate are sent along nerve fibers to the olfactory bulb. This is a structure at the front of the brain, located just above the nose. Here, the signals are processed and routed to the areas of the brain where smells are processed.

Tastes

The sense of taste begins with the taste buds. These are collections of cells on the tongue that detect flavor molecules. Nerves carry signals from the taste buds to the brainstem. From there, they go to the hypothalamus, the thalamus and the sensory cortex's taste center.

Investigate

Sometimes the brain can be tricked by the information sent to it by the eyes. The brain always tries to "make sense" of the messages it gets, and sometimes this leads it into making mistakes about what is actually there. These visual tricks are called optical illusions and some are great fun. See how many you can find. There are lots of websites that are devoted to optical, or visual, illusions.

Contact senses

There are millions upon millions of specialized nerves beneath the surface of the skin. They provide us with a mass of information about the objects we touch. This stream of information is fed back to a part of the brain called the somatosensory cortex. Here, the characteristics of the object are interpreted as hot or cold, hard or soft, wet or dry, and so on.

Receptor gallery

Beneath your skin there are remarkable arrays of receptors. These are parts of cells that detect changes in the surroundings. They are constantly monitoring and reporting on conditions around you. Here are the five different types of receptor and what they do.

Bulbs of Krause: tiny capsules containing many branched nerve endings. These detect fast changes in the skin shape caused by vibrations and pressure changes, such as air moving on the skin.

Meissner's endings: found especially in the skin on the hands, feet, lips, and the inner eyelids. They can detect very light touches and vibrations.

Pacinian endings: buried deep beneath the skin, these detect heavy pressure and fast vibrations.

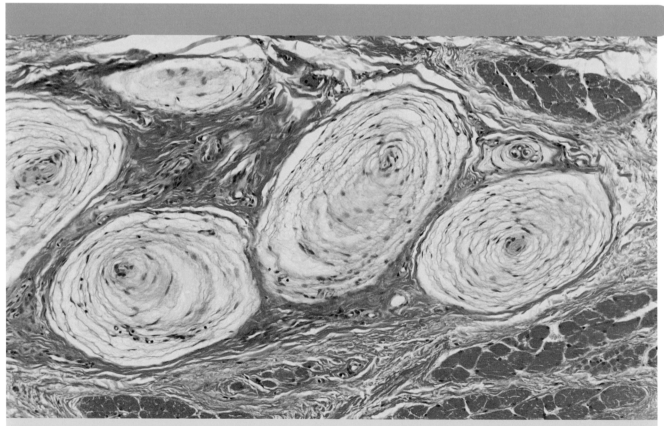

32

This is a photomicrograph of Pacinian endings in the skin. These receptors are sensitive to touch and vibration.

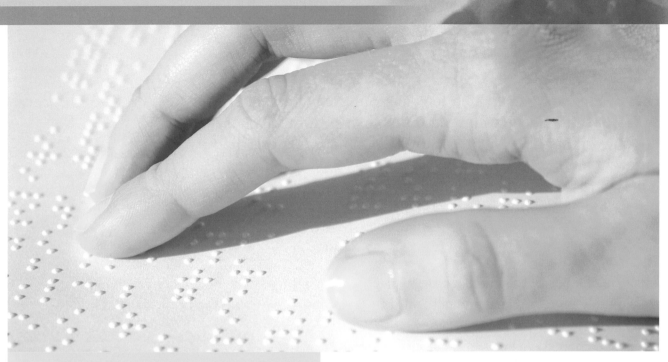

The sensitive touch sensors in the fingertips allow a blind person to read the patterns of bumps that make up the Braille alphabet.

Merkel's endings: these look like tiny disks on the underside of the skin. They can detect very light touches.

Ruffini endings: these respond to continued pressure on the skin.

Free nerve endings: these are simply branching nerve fibers and are the most common of the skin's detectors. They respond to heat, cold, light touches, and heavy pressure—it is these nerve endings that signal when something is painful.

The somatosensory cortex

The somatosensory cortex is located in a strip across the center of the brain, running from left to right. When the skin is touched, signals from the millions of sensors beneath its surface trigger the neurons of the somatosensory cortex.

Different areas of the body are allocated different areas of the somatosensory cortex, according to how sensitive to touch they are. For example, the area dealing with the fingers is much bigger than that dealing with the shoulders.

Try this

Take a paper clip and bend it into a U shape with the tips about 0.8 in. (2 cm) apart. Lightly touch the ends of the paper clip to the back of a partner's hand and ask if he or she felt one touch or two. If the answer is two, push the points a little closer together and try again. When only one touch is reported, measure the distance between the points. Repeat the process with another part of the body. The parts that can detect two points at the shortest distance apart, are those with the most touch detectors.

Who are you?

One of the most remarkable things about being human is having a sense of self—being aware of ourselves as individuals. Research has shown that different areas of the brain are responsible for different mental functions. Like computers linked together across a network, these different areas share information with each other. Somehow, from this sharing, there emerges a person.

The frontal lobes

The frontal lobes of the brain appear to play a major role in determining the personality, particularly the part of the lobes known as the prefrontal cortex. We know this because there is evidence of personality changes in people who have suffered frontal lobe injuries.

Emotion

Emotions are a crucial part of who we are. They signal our likes and dislikes, our loves and our fears. Strong emotion can have an effect on the whole body. It can bring tears to our eyes, make our palms sweat, and our hearts race. Emotions appear to be triggered from deep down in the brain, especially from the hypothalamus.

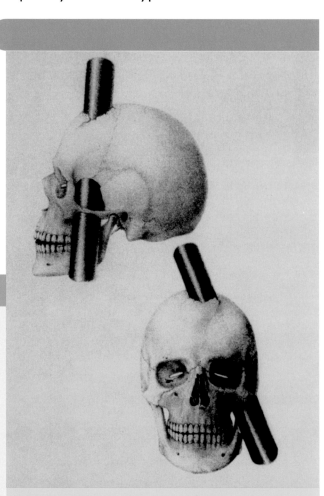

These drawings show how the metal rod passed through the skull of Phineas Gage. Gage's injuries were so severe that he was lucky not to have been killed instantly.

Body facts

Phineas Gage was a railroad worker in Vermont. In 1848, a freak accident sent a metal rod through his left cheek and out through the top of his skull, causing severe injury to the prefrontal cortex. Gage survived, but people noticed a great change in his personality. Once efficient and easy-going, he became an ill-tempered and foul-mouthed man who was unable to stick to a plan. His friends said he was "no longer Gage."

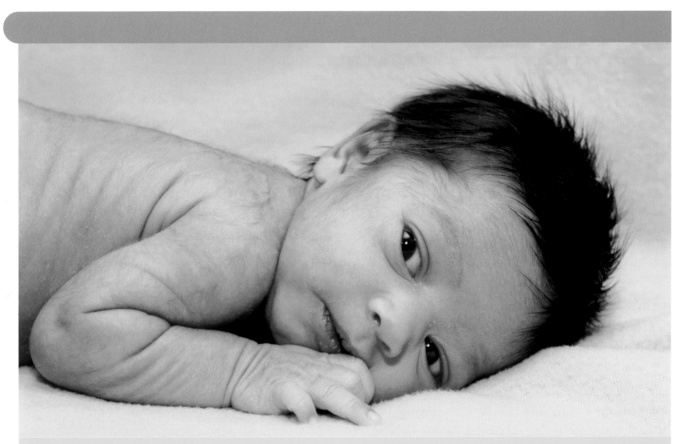

How much of our personality is present at birth and how much is it affected by our experiences? No one really knows.

The amgydala and hippocampus, together with the hypothalamus, form part of the brain's limbic system (see page 21). They are also involved in emotion and play a part in self-awareness—the understanding that one exists as an individual, separate from other people.

Both the amgydala and hippocampus are involved in the formation and storage of memories. In some ways, it could be said that our memories make us who we are. Often, it is remembering things that happened in the past that determines how we react to something in the present.

Investigate

Self awareness, sometimes also called sentience, is something that we still struggle to understand. Are humans the only sentient creatures, or are other animals, such as dogs and dolphins, sentient, too? Will it be possible to build a sentient computer? See what you can find out about animal sentience.

Drugs and the brain

There are drugs that can be used to change our moods by altering the chemistry of the brain. Some people are prescribed these drugs to help them to deal with problems such as depression. But people don't only take mood-altering drugs for medical reasons—some take them for recreation. When people take drugs, what is actually happening in the brain?

Changing the balance

Most drugs work by changing the chemical balance at the synapses of the brain cells. For instance, the antidepressant drug fluoxetine works by increasing the activity of serotonin. Serotonin is a neurotransmitter that increases the frequency of signals being passed between neurons. This helps to improve the mood of someone suffering from depression.

Tranquillizers are drugs used to treat anxiety and insomnia (difficulty in falling or staying asleep). They act to increase the production of the chemical in the brain that reduces neuron activity. This can calm people down and help them sleep. Some drugs prescribed for depression produce surges of a neurotransmitter called dopamine. When dopamine is released in the brain, it produces a feeling of pleasure.

Alcohol

People all over the world have made and consumed alcohol for thousands of years. In many societies, alcohol abuse has caused major health and social problems.

Alcohol can get into the bloodstream and reach the brain very rapidly. It acts on many sites in the nervous system, including the spinal cord, the cerebellum, and the cerebral cortex. It also

Depression is a serious and crippling medical condition, but it can often be treated by the use of appropriate drugs.

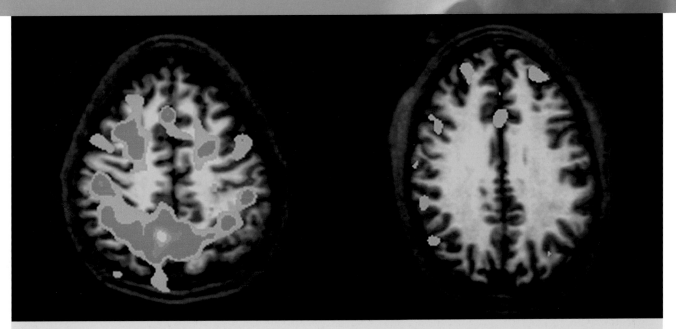

Two brain scans: on the left, the red areas show activity in a normal brain during problem-solving; on the right, we can see reduced activity in the brain of an alcoholic asked to solve the same problem.

interferes with many neurotransmitters. Persistent alcohol use can lead to damage to the frontal lobes, with neurotransmitter levels being reduced and fewer connections between neurons. It can also result in the actual loss of neurons.

Smart drugs

Can you imagine being able to take a pill that would tune your brain, like tuning the engine of a high-performance car? Today, people are actually conducting research into substances that might just make it possible to do that.

Chemicals called "cognitive enhancers," or "smart drugs," are being studied in laboratories. These smart drugs could have several effects. For example, they might improve the ability to learn and to memorize things. They could also increase levels of concentration and aid in problem-solving, planning, and decision-making.

In most cases, so far, cognitive enhancers have been used to treat people with neurological problems or mental disorders. However, growing numbers of healthy people want to make themselves smarter by taking cognitive enhancers. So far, there is little evidence to show that these drugs would really work on them. Further tests need to be conducted on healthy people before taking these smart drugs becomes the smart thing to do.

Investigate

Alcohol can be a very dangerous drug. Drinking too much of it can damage the brain and other vital body organs. In addition, people can become dependent on the effects of alcohol. See what you can find out about this legal but potentially harmful drug.

Brain damage

The brain, as we have seen, is a vital part of the body. It controls our movements and interprets our senses. It also provides us with understanding and the ability to learn. Injury to the brain can cause problems with some or all of these functions.

The skull

The brain is held within the protective bone of the skull. It is cushioned by a jellylike material and a layer of cerebrospinal fluid that provides support while also acting as a shock absorber. The outer surface of the skull is smooth, but the inner surface is rough and jagged. This rough inner surface can cause damage if sudden jarring movements cause the brain to hit against the inside of the skull.

Brain injuries

Any severe blow to the head can cause injury to the brain. Neurons in the brain are not replaced. Because of this, brain damage can have lifelong physical and mental consequences.

Wearing a bicycle helmet can help to prevent damage to the skull and brain if a cyclist is involved in an accident.

If the head is hit with sufficient force, the brain turns and twists around the brainstem. This interrupts normal nerve pathways and results in unconsciousness. An injured person who remains unconscious for a long period of time is said to be in a coma.

Closed head injury

The term *closed head injury* is used when the brain has been damaged without actual damage to the skull. One example of this is shaken baby syndrome, in which severe and violent shaking of the head can cause damage to large areas of the brain. The results can include paralysis, problems with behavior and learning, persistent vegetative state, and death.

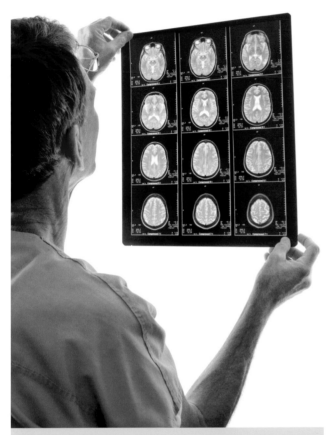

A doctor carefully examines MRI brain scans for any sign of damage.

The body can be affected in a number of ways, depending on how severe the damage is and exactly where it is located.

In a car accident where the head comes into sudden impact with a hard surface, multiple areas of the brain are damaged. The brain rebounds forward and backward against the skull. This tears blood vessels and causes damage to the temporal lobes as they rub against the inside of the skull.

Investigate

Do you know what to do if you see someone injure their head? Head injuries can be serious and the person should not be moved. They should be examined by a doctor as soon as possible. A head wound might mean a skull fracture and possible injury to the brain.

Symptoms of brain injury can include loss of consciousness or confusion, and blurred vision or seeing double. The person may experience dizziness, ringing in the ears, and have trouble thinking clearly.

Fun facts

Brain weights

Sperm whale—17 lb. (7.8 kg)
Elephant—10.5 lb. (4.8 kg)
Adult human—46–50 oz. (1.3–1.4 kg)
Giraffe—24 oz. (680 g)
Cow—16 oz. (450 g)
Lion—8.5 oz. (240 g)
Sheep—5 oz. (140 g)
Great white shark—1.2 oz. (34 g)
Rabbit—0.4 oz. (12 g)
Guinea pig—0.14 oz. (4 g)
Goldfish—0.004 oz. (0.1 g)

Shutting down

You will lose consciousness within 8 to 10 seconds of a loss of blood supply to the brain.

I don't get it ...

It seems there's a place for humor in your brain. People with damage to the right side of their frontal lobe just can't tell why a punchline is supposed to be funny.

Elephants never forget

Scientists confirmed this old saying while studying three herds of elephants in a national park in Tanzania during a drought. When the drought hit, two of the herds left the park led by matriarchs (lead female elephants) who were around 40 years old. These matriarchs had survived a severe drought 35 years earlier and remembered where to migrate to in order to survive. The members of the herd that remained were too young to experience the previous drought. Sadly, this herd lost 40 percent of its calves, but over 90 percent of the calves in the other herds survived, thanks to the matriarchs' long-term memory.

Moth-robot

Scientists have built a robot controlled by a moth's brain. An electrode is attached to the vision center of the moth's brain, so the moth's eye movements steer the robot.

Bright spark!

The brain uses about 12 watts of power—less than the light inside your refrigerator.

Just can't get it out of my head

Ever wondered why some songs get stuck in your head? We're very good at remembering the sequences of things we see and do regularly,

The legendary elephant's memory has a basis in fact.

like the order of the channels on television, signing our names, or how to make a pot of tea. A song with a good hook takes advantage of this sequence recall ability. The more you think about it, the more the nerve pathways associated with it are strengthened, making it even more likely that you'll think about it again.

Einstein's brain

The brain of the genius scientist, Albert Einstein, was removed shortly after he died in 1955. Einstein's brain had an unusual pattern of grooves on the part of the brain that is thought to be important for mathematical abilities. His brain was also 15 percent wider than other brains studied. Researchers think that these unique brain features may have allowed better connections between brain cells used in mathematics.

Big baby

If a baby's weight increased at the same rate as the number of connections between its brain cells increases, then by the time it was a month old, it would weigh 170 pounds (77 kilograms).

Eye say!

An ostrich's eye is actually bigger than its brain.

Stack them up

If you made a stack of paper with one sheet for each of the 100,000 million neurons in your brain, it would reach a staggering 5,000 miles (8,000 kilometers) high.

Pain in the brain

Your brain feels no pain—there are no pain-detecting nerve cells in the brain itself. This

The ostrich has the largest eyes of any land animal, but its brain is very small in proportion to its body.

means that surgeons can perform brain operations on patients who are fully conscious.

Around the world

If all of the blood vessels in your brain were laid out in a line, they would be long enough to circle the world four times.

What's that?

You may have heard of *déjà vu*—the feeling that something new has been experienced before. But have you heard of *jamais vu*—"never seen"—the feeling that you no longer know something you used to know, such as your phone number, or the name of your favorite actor? Scientists are still trying to work out what causes these strange memory experiences.

Activities

The Stroop Effect

In the 1930s, the psychologist, J. Ridley Stroop, discovered a strange thing about the workings of the brain that has come to be called the "Stroop Effect." Look at the list of words in the panel at the bottom of this page and name their colors. Don't read the actual word, say the color it is. For example, if the word "yellow" is written in blue, don't say "yellow," say "blue." You'll find it harder than you think.

We are so influenced by words that the brain gets confused when there is a word/color mismatch. When you look at the color, your brain cannot help reading the word, and it struggles to work out the correct answer. This may be because your brain reads words faster than it is able to name colors.

The test can be influenced by several factors, including lack of sleep, minor brain injury, and

Investigate

What do you think would happen if:

• you turned the words upside down?

• you used words that are not colors, such as "cat" or "dog"?

• you tried the experiment with a young child who had not yet learned to read?

Now perform the experiments and find out if you were right.

high altitudes. Each of these will increase the time that it takes for a person to complete the test. In fact, the test has been used on mountain climbing expeditions to see how high altitudes affect different people.

GREEN   ORANGE   BLUE

RED   VIOLET   BLACK

GREY   YELLOW   BEIGE

WHITE   PURPLE   PINK

Card games can be an excellent way of strengthening your memory and powers of deduction.

The memory game

From a pack of playing cards, take 15 matched pairs of cards. Shuffle the cards and lay them face down on a table. One player begins by turning over two of the cards. If the cards match, for example, if they are both sevens, the player removes the pair and turns over two more. If the cards don't match, they are turned face down again in their original positions. Then it is the next player's turn.

The object of the game is to remember where the cards are located and to pick up as many pairs as possible. When all the pairs have been found, the winner is the person with the most pairs.

The game can be made more difficult by using all 52 cards in the pack. You can also play the game on your own, making it your aim to clear the table in the fewest number of turns. Games like this can help improve your memory.

Glossary

Antidepressant a drug used to treat depression

Auditory related to hearing

Autonomic ganglion a cluster of cell bodies that is a junction point between autonomic nerves from the central nervous system and autonomic nerves that stimulate the target muscle

Axon an extension of a neuron (nerve cell) that transmits outgoing signals from one nerve cell body to another; each neuron has one axon

Cell body the central part of a neuron that contains its nucleus and other essential cell structures, and from which the axon and dendrites extend

Cerebrospinal fluid a colorless, clear watery fluid that surrounds the brain and spinal cord

Connective tissue body tissue that holds together and supports organs and other structures in the body

Cortex the outer layer of the cerebrum; it is densely packed with nerve cell bodies

Dendrite extensions from a neuron cell body that receive signals arriving from other neurons

Glial cells specialized cells that surround nerve cells and perform various supporting functions for them

Gray matter nerve tissue that appears grayish in color, because it is mostly made up of nerve cell bodies

Meninges membranes that enclose and protect the brain and spinal cord

Motor neuron a neuron that carries impulses from the brain or spinal cord to a muscle, triggering it to contract

Myelin a fatty, insulating sheath that encloses axons aiding the efficient conduction of nerve impulses along the neuron

Neuroanatomy the study of the structure and function of the nervous system

Neurological having to do with the nervous system

Neuron a nerve cell, a cell specialized to carry information from one part of the body to another

Neurotransmitter one of a group of chemicals that carries nerve signals from one nerve cell to another across the synapse

Nucleus the part of a cell that contains its genetic material

Olfactory related to the sense of smell

Receptor part of a cell that detects and responds to some kind of outside stimulation

REM rapid eye movement, a period of light sleep during which the eyes can be seen to move rapidly back and forth beneath the lids; dreams take place during REM sleep

Sensory neuron a neuron that carries information to the brain and spinal cord from other parts of the body

Synapse a tiny gap between two nerve cells, where a nerve impulse passes from one nerve cell, or neuron, to another

White matter nerve tissue that appears pale in color because it is mostly made up of nerve axons

Further Information and Web Sites

The Brain and Nervous System by Carol Ballard (KidHaven Press, 2005)

The Great Brain Book: An Inside Look At The Inside Of Your Head by H. P. Newquist (Scholastic Reference, 2005)

What Happens When You Move? by Jacqui Bailey (PowerKids Press, 2008)

Web Sites
Due to the changing nature of Internet links, Rosen Publishing has developed an online list of Web Sites related to the subject of this book. This site is regularly updated. Please use this link to access this list: http://www.rosenlinks.com/uhb/brain

Index